Facebook Influencer Guide

How to become a Facebook influencer, work with influencers and how to monetize your facebook business - for beginners

By Jeff Abston

Copyright © 2018 Jeff Abston

All rights reserved.

ISBN: 1985665549

ISBN-13: 978-1985665545

© Copyright 2018 by Jeff Abston - All rights reserved.

This document is geared towards providing exact and reliable information in regard to the topic and issues covered. The publication is sold with the idea that the publisher is not required to render accounting, officially permitted, or otherwise, qualified services. If advice is necessary, legal or professional, a practiced individual in the profession should be ordered.

- From a Declaration of Principles which was accepted and approved equally by a Committee of the American Bar Association and a Committee of Publishers and Associations.

In no way is it legal to reproduce, duplicate, or transmit any part of this document in either electronic means or in printed format. Recording of this publication is strictly prohibited and any storage of this document is not allowed unless with written permission from the publisher. All rights reserved.

The information provided herein is stated to be truthful and consistent, in that any liability, in terms of inattention or otherwise, by any usage or abuse of any policies, processes, or directions contained within is the solitary and utter responsibility of the recipient reader. Under no circumstances will any legal responsibility or blame be held against the publisher for any reparation, damages, or monetary loss due to the information herein, either directly or indirectly.

Respective authors own all copyrights not held by the publisher.

The information herein is offered for informational purposes solely and is universal as such. The presentation of the information is without contract or any type of guarantee or assurance.

Table of Contents

INTRODUCTION 1

FACEBOOK INFLUENCER 3

Why Facebook? 3

How to Find Facebook Influencers 5

Ideas for Facebook Influencer Marketing 8

THE BEGINNER'S GUIDE TO INFLUENCER MARKETING ON FACEBOOK 13

How to Find Influencers on Facebook 13

WAYS TO FASTER INFLUENCE MARKETING .. 18

Ways to Increase Your Facebook Fan Page Influence 19

SOCIAL MEDIA & INFLUENCER MARKETING.27

5 Steps to Hack Your Facebook Influencer Marketing Campaign 29

WAYS SOCIAL MEDIA INFLUENCERS CAN GROW YOUR BRAND 33

REASONS WHY INFLUENCER MARKETING IS GOOD FOR YOUR BUSINESS 37

WHO IS AN INFLUENCER? 38

WHY SHOULD YOUR BUSINESS CONSIDER INFLUENCER MARKETING? 39

THE BENEFITS OF SOCIAL INFLUENCER MARKETING .. 41

THE IMPORTANCE OF SOCIAL MEDIA INFLUENCERS 46
STEPS TO EFFECTIVE INFLUENCER MARKETING 50
In-depth: What is an influencer and what does he/she do? .. 51
Sector Influencers 52
Ranking influencers 56
Working with influencers: 57
Build influencers: 60
THE ESSENCE OF INFLUENCER FOR BUSINESS GROWTH 61
Offer Exposure 63
Ask For Advice 63
Hire As A Spokesperson or Speaker 64
Pay For A Product Review 64
CONCLUSION 65

INTRODUCTION

Facebook is the single best place for business influencers to connect authentically with people and reach new audiences. Hundreds of global business leaders across industries, regions and enterprises use Facebook, with more signing up every day. Facebook gives these leaders the opportunity for direct communication with complete control over their messages, precision targeting, and a flexible set of publishing tools, including text, photos, videos, live video, and more.

The term "influencer" is wiggling its way through a tangled web, and it's a hard one to catch because no one knows for certain what it looks like. Personally, I think this is where the biggest challenge lies, because an influencer is like a changeling. It has a different image for every brand and often for every brand campaign.

If you want to become a recognized figure in your business market, it's time to get out of your introverted lifestyle and become the established "that guy" or "that gal" whose opinions are revered by the public. Nevertheless, this won't be achieved overnight and certainly not at all if you're unwilling to take action.

Networking is a straight-forward skill that can be applied simultaneously in real life and in business. One of the most simplified strategies to network and connect with your audience online is through Facebook. For business purposes, you need to create a fan page and optimize it with your contact information, local area keywords, hours of operation and website URL.

Subsequently, you will observe that you don't have any followers or "likes". How discouraging. After all the blood, sweat and tears you put into your business it can be very depressing to see such a small social presence. This is the foundation of evolving and flourishing your business influence.

Once you realize the number of loyal fans increasing, place a Facebook badge on your website showing the number of people who have "liked" your page. Place a congratulations message on your wall to the 500th person to like your page. Hold a contest to reach 1,000 fans.

These increasing numbers are considered social proof that what you have to say is tremendously substantial and why many people consider you an expert - because they are following you.

Keep in mind, networking is NOT selling. It's fundamentally an introduction to others in your area who might need your products or services at some point in the future. If you make a good impression and network on a consistent basis, people will remember you fondly and recommend you.

FACEBOOK INFLUENCER

One of the first questions that comes to mind when you plan an influencer marketing campaign is which platform are you going to use. You know you want to use social media channels for your campaign, but you're not sure which of them will deliver the best results.

If you're still thinking about it, maybe you should consider Facebook influencer marketing and/or Instagram influencer marketing. Facebook and Instagram are the top choices when it comes to social media influencer marketing.

Each of them has their unique benefits. In this post, you're going to learn all about Facebook influencer marketing. You will find out why Facebook is such a great choice, how to find influencers for the platform, and how to execute your campaign.

Why Facebook?

Facebook is an excellent platform for executing your influencer marketing campaign for several reasons. Here are some of the best:

1. Popularity

Facebook continues to be the most popular social media channel, according to the Pew Research Center. Statista reports that the platform has 1.94 billion active users on a monthly basis making it the most widely-used social media channel with a high chance of finding your target audience. With such a massive user base, Facebook gives you the opportunity to reach a bigger audience for your influencer marketing campaign.

2. Engagement

In addition to being highly popular, Facebook also attracts an engaged audience. Out of the almost 2 billion users, at least 1.25 billion of them log onto the platform every day, according to another Statista study. A Mediakix study found that each user spends around 35 minutes of their day on the platform, just five minutes shorter than YouTube.

3. Influencer Preference

So Facebook influencer marketing allows you to reach a huge and engaged audience. But that's not the only reason why you should consider a Facebook influencer marketing campaign. According to a Bloglovin study, Facebook is the second most preferred platform among influencers themselves. They consider it almost as effective as Instagram in executing an influencer marketing campaign.

These are some of the top reasons why Facebook influencer marketing is such an excellent choice for your brand. You can see that not only will you reach a massive audience through the platform, but these consumers would be highly engaged. And then you'll also be executing the campaign in a platform preferred by influencers.

How to Find Facebook Influencers

Now that you understand the benefits of Facebook influencer marketing, it's time you find influencers to work with on your campaign. But finding influencers on Facebook is a little more challenging than on other platforms because of the content restrictions and privacy laws.

Use these tips to make your search easier and find ideal Facebook influencers to work with:

1. Keyword Research on Facebook

If you're conducting your search using the Facebook platform, you should ideally look for pages and not individual accounts. For your campaign to have the optimum impact, everyone should be able to access the influencer's content easily. The privacy settings for individual accounts can make that challenging.

To find influencers for Facebook influencer marketing, you need to choose relevant keywords related to your brand, product or industry. For example, if you want to promote your product through influential social media parents, you can choose keywords like "parenting," "parent," "mother," etc.

As you can see in the screenshot below, the search results for parenting pages will not show a lot of influential individuals at the top. While some brands still choose to work with these influential pages, you may want a more humanized, person-to-person impact.

If this is the case, you can further filter the results by selecting the "artist, band or public figure" category. Once you do this, you'll get more accurate results for parenting guide authors and experts at parenting.

2. Using HYPR

A manual research for influencers on Facebook can be time-consuming, but it's necessary if you have budget limitations and can't invest in a tool. However, if you can afford to invest some money in effective influencer marketing tools, HYPR is an excellent option as well as Influencer Marketing Consultant.

The good thing about HYPR is that it won't just track the stats of an influencer on Twitter. It will also pull up the influencer's data from other social media channels including Facebook. So you can easily find relevant Facebook users with significant influence on the platform.

As you can see in the screenshot below, HYPR will show you the number of followers the influencer has on Facebook and it will also show the number of likes, comments, and shares they get on the platform. The tool gives you a breakdown of demographics of the influencer's audience base. This makes it even simpler for you to find influencers according to your target audience.

3. Insight pool

Insight pool is another useful tool for finding influencers across social media platforms. Through this platform, you can not only find Facebook influencers but also get complete insight into their social media activity. This will help you further filter influencers based on the type of content they create/share.

In the screenshot below, the tool displays all the topics in which the influencer specializes. You will also be able to see the history of brands she's worked with and how she helped execute the campaigns.

These are some of the best ways to find influencers for your Facebook influencer marketing campaign. If you find influencer research a hassle, you can work with influencer marketing agencies. These agencies will put you in touch with some of the best and most relevant influencers for your brand. They will do the research and communication work for you to successfully execute your campaign.

Ideas for Facebook Influencer Marketing

You know the importance of launching a Facebook influencer marketing campaign. You also know how to find the influencers to work with. Now let's take a look at some of the best tactics for launching a Facebook influencer marketing campaign.

1. Sharing Experiences through Facebook Live

You might have heard that Facebook videos are an engaging form of content. But what's even more engaging is the platform's live video. Facebook reports that their users spend three times longer watching these live video feeds than watching regular videos.

So if you want to engage your target audience through Facebook influencers, get your influencers to go Live. Through Facebook Live, influencers can share their experiences with your brand or product. They might broadcast themselves using your product or trying it out for the first time. They could broadcast a live video of their experience visiting your store or even an event you've hosted. There are endless opportunities to use Facebook Live in your Facebook influencer marketing campaign.

An excellent example is how the Best Fiends video game developers partnered with influential figures, who have more than 3 million Facebook fans. Laura engaged with her fans through live stream and demonstrated how to play the game. But she and her husband also followed her usual storyline by playing their usual characters from her other videos – Pamela and Roger. They managed to keep things fun and interesting while still promoting the video game. The video has received 9000 comments and 8,300 reactions to date. It has been shared more than 800 times. This shows that the influencer was able to efficiently engage a significant amount of people through the Facebook Live video.

2. Cross-Promoting Campaign from Other Platforms

Even if you are already finding success with influencer marketing on other platforms, Facebook gives you the opportunity to further improve the performance of your campaign. For example, maybe you're already running a campaign in which influencers create a blog post about your products. You can get them to promote the content through Facebook as well to gain optimum reach.

This is how the influencers for Minnie & Maxxie ensured better results for their brand awareness campaign. Scrunch conducted a case study and found that cross-promoting the campaign on various platforms results in high levels of engagement and exposure.

The brand provided a select few fashion and style influencers with exclusive access to their products. These influencers helped raise awareness for the new line of products through Instagram. To get optimized reach and engagement, they also cross promoted the content through Facebook. Here's an example of a post by twin bloggers, Nicole and Danielle of When Words Fail.

The brand worked with 19 influencers, each of whom shared photos of the brand's products with their social media followers on Instagram and Facebook. The campaign saw almost 18,500 direct engagements with the influencer content. By using Facebook, the campaign was able to expand their reach to 433,445.

3. Standing Up for a Cause

Cause marketing has been among the favorite marketing tools for brands for a good reason. It is an effective way to humanize your brand. It's a way to show your audience that you care about certain issues – whether social, political, or environmental. Putting influencer into the mix further enhances the effectiveness of your cause marketing campaign.

So when you're planning to execute a Facebook influencer marketing campaign, try to get them to promote a cause you support. For Joseph Gordon-Levitt, it was easier to execute an influencer cause marketing campaign for his company, Hit Record, because he could play the role of an influencer.

Hit Record partnered with Find Your Park, a cause that promotes the conservation of America's national parks. Hit Record helped the cause by designing branded merchandise. Joseph Gordon-Levitt then promoted the products through his Facebook page. By doing this, he's helping promote the cause while establishing his company as one that supports it.

4. Promoting Giveaway Contests

Facebook is an excellent channel for promoting a giveaway contest through influencers. Your Facebook influencer marketing campaign may revolve around raising awareness for your brand and boosting brand engagement. In this case, you can come up with a contest that the influencer can host on their blog or you can host on your website.

The influencers will then promote the contest on Facebook by sharing a link to the page. Giveaway contests work well in engaging a new audience because there's something in it for them. They would gladly engage with your brand if there's a chance they'll get something beneficial from it.

Ziera Footwear nailed this tactic by combining it with cause marketing for their Unstoppable Women campaign. The brand ran a giveaway campaign through relevant fashion influencers like Katherine Saab of Stylendipity. The blogger hosted the contest on her blog and then promoted it through her Facebook page.

5. Telling Stories Using Videos

Video content consumption is increasing on Facebook, which makes videos perfect for telling your brand story through influencers. TechCrunch reported in 2015 that Facebook users watch an average of 8 million videos in a day. Recode also reports that people watch 100 million hours of Facebook video every day.

This makes it clear that video content is crucial for engaging Facebook users. The Viral Nation case study of a Crayola influencer marketing campaign is an excellent example. The goal of the campaign was to build buzz before the launch of the new Crayola Air Marker Sprayer.

Crayola worked with social media influencers to tell unique stories using videos. While some influencers created videos explaining what they can use the product for, others put a comical twist to the content. Your Everyday Canadian, for example, created a funny video in which he uses the sprayer to make money for pizza. This video has been viewed 577,000 times, and has received almost 800 reactions. The campaign generated a total of 4 million engagements with 7.1 million impressions.

THE BEGINNER'S GUIDE TO INFLUENCER MARKETING ON FACEBOOK

You're planning to execute an influencer marketing campaign on social media. The problem is, you're not sure which social media platform you should use or how to get started.

Facebook continues to be the most popular social media network worldwide. It's also the favorite platform of nearly one-third of influencers in the US for sharing branded content, followed by Instagram.

A Mavrck study found that when influencers and other users post about a brand on Facebook, it drives 6.9 times more engagement than content posted by the brands themselves. An incredible 95.8% of social media marketers worldwide say that Facebook offers the best ROI.

How to Find Influencers on Facebook

The biggest challenge is finding influencers on Facebook. Unlike with Instagram and Twitter, Facebook has some content restrictions and privacy terms that can make it more difficult to find influential profiles or pages. Here are some of the best ways to find top Facebook influencers:

1. Use Tools to Find Facebook Influencers

Tools like Simply Measured can help you find top social media influencers on Facebook and other platforms. These tools will help you search for influencers using a relevant keyword.

Listening-4 Influencer. These tools will show you social media stats about each influencer, like the number of Facebook followers they have, their social media activity, and how they relate to your target audience.

2. Find Facebook Influencers through Agencies

In addition to these tools, there are other options for connecting with Facebook influencers for your campaign. You can find agencies that will connect you with some of the most relevant and effective influencers for your business, based on your requirements.

Some of these influencer marketing agencies will provide you with in-depth insights and other relevant industry data. As part of a campaign with Viral Nation, for example, they will provide you with audience retention and viewership rates, paid vs. organic viewership, impressions and other key insights. Based on these insights, you can easily track the performance of your campaign and make changes or adjustments as needed.

What's great about working with an agency is that they can handle the time-consuming aspects, like research and communication for you. Many brands find it challenging to connect with the influencers they like because they are very busy. But through an agency, you can leave all the proposals and communication tasks to the experts.

Facebook Influencer Marketing Ideas

Now that you've identified the best influencers to work with for your campaign, it's time to get started with Facebook influencer marketing. For this, you can help ensure the success of your campaign by using some of the most effective tactics. Here are three of the most effective influencer marketing strategies for Facebook:

1. Have Influencers Tell a Story through Video

According to Recode, Facebook users watch 100 million hours of video on the platform every day. TechCrunch reports that Facebook users watched an average of 8 billion videos daily. This can only mean one thing: video content can be an excellent mode for marketing your brand with Facebook influencers.

You can get influencers to tell a story about your brand or products using Facebook videos. They can also share their experiences, for example, the unboxing of your product. Facebook video content created by influencers can effectively engage your target audience, which can enhance the effectiveness of your campaign.

Your Everyday Canadian created a Facebook video telling a funny story about the product. To date, the video has been viewed 577K times, and has gotten 790 likes, 199 shares, and 60 comments. Out of the 577K views, 498,703 were unique viewers, and nearly half

(41.9%) of the views ended up with completion. The video has generated a total of 1,133,977 impressions.

Overall, the Crayola influencer marketing campaign generated 4 million engagements and 7.1 million impressions. The campaign also drove so much traffic to the official Crayola website that it ended up crashing.

2. Have Influencers Share an Experience through Facebook Live

Although Facebook videos already drive a lot of engagement, it can be even better for your influencer marketing campaign. According to Facebook, users spend three times longer watching Facebook Live videos than regular videos.

So if you want to enhance the engagement rate of your influencer marketing campaign, have your influencers go Live to share their experiences.

The experience could be anything from an unboxing, a first look, or even an event that your brand has organized. Many brands and marketers have implemented Facebook Live videos into their influencer marketing campaigns with impressive results. The best part about Live videos is that the video is still available for viewing even after the end of the campaign.

The Best Fiends video game, for example, promoted the game through influencers like Laura Clery. She created a Facebook Live video, which has received 467K views and 8.3K reactions. The video has been shared more than 800 times and has received over 9,000 comments

3. Have Influencers Promote a Contest

Contests are an excellent way for brands to promote themselves. Since there's a chance for people to win something, they will readily engage with your brand, even if they haven't heard of you before. Contests can help you raise brand awareness in ways you can't even imagine. And with the help of influencers, you can further optimize this tactic to reach a much wider audience.

Send out some free goodies to Facebook influencers so they can host a giveaway contest, or have them promote a contest you're hosting on your site. They could post photos of the products and include a link to your contest page.

These are some of the best ways you can work with influencers to market your brand on Facebook. As you can see, it's important to find the right influencers, and then run campaigns to effectively engage your target audience.

WAYS TO FASTER INFLUENCE MARKETING

I recently discovered that there are actual websites that allow people and or companies to purchase Facebook "likes" and/or Twitter followers. (Apparently there is a popularity contest going on and I have not been in the loop.) Initially, I thought to myself, "What a weird concept, having to buy friends. Why would anyone pay for that?" Then I realized that while Facebook for me is strictly for social reasons (keeping in touch with actual friends), many people use it as a branding service. Whether they are branding themselves, their company or another company, such social sites provide a forum to build a name and market it to a wide range of people. They use it as a means of influencer marketing themselves.

We all know word of mouth influence is still one of the most effective types of marketing, and social media allows this at a greater depth. Rather than telling your neighbor about the new iPad you just purchased, in hopes of him spreading the news, you can just post it on Facebook and right away it will appear on the home page of all 300 of your friends. There is actual proof of it. Now imagine purchasing 300 more friends, which means another 300 people have now read your Facebook status and have one way or another been socially influenced by it. It's not that you paid for the people; you merely paid for the time you saved from having to go and befriend ANOTHER 300 people.

However you view this idea of "buying influence," it does not take away from its effectiveness. And as I have mentioned in previous blogs, the social media world moves fast and you have to keep up or you will be left behind.

Ways to Increase Your Facebook Fan Page Influence

As a business owner, you probably understand the importance of having a strong and visible presence in the social media world. Facebook is the highest ranking website in the world, and it is therefore important to your business' success that you learn how to best tap into this expansive market.

The good news is that Facebook makes it pretty easy to establish a strong Internet following with its fan page feature. A Facebook page is a great way to interact with existing customers, advertise your business in the world's largest market, get new prospects and grow your business. The next most important step to creating a Facebook fan page is learning how to use it to its full capacity, and this begins with learning how to make your page visible to as many people as possible.

Here are four ways to increase your Facebook influence:

1. Be active. It's quite simple: if you want to increase your fan page's visibility, you have to participate on other fan pages. Make it a point to "like" other, related fan pages, and then browse their walls and photos and interact with their fans in a way that will get you some attention. When you make the effort to participate on other fan pages, they tend to reciprocate, and their fans notice and jump on board.

2. Post valuable content. No one will be happy getting spammed by your fan page ten times a day with the same promotional message. If you really want to gain loyal fans who are inspired to send more fans to you, then you need to provide valuable information. Take your time to plan and prepare entertaining, interesting and informative posts. Post them consistently and at the same time every day so your fans know what to expect from you.

3. Spreading the word. Include the link to your Facebook fan page on all your business communications. This includes your website, business cards, email signatures, letterheads, and advertisements.

4. Ask for help. Once you have proven to your fans that you are committed to provide them with quality posts and genuine interactions, you should have loyal fans who will be willing to help you out. Don't be afraid to ask them to recommend you to friends and share your status updates, posts, and pictures.

How to Win Facebook Friends and Influence Tweeple

Ever wonder why some don't work and play well with others on Facebook and Twitter? Social media is like a virtual party where almost the same rules apply as they do in face-to-face communication. But many people mistakenly think that since it's online, it's OK to bend those social rules for social media. Nothing could be further from the truth. Here are some do's and don'ts...OK here are the don'ts! If you do the opposite, there are your do's.

1. Don't expect everyone to come to you

If you build it, they won't necessarily come. Just like you cannot put up a website and expect a flood of customers to drop money in your account. You can't build a Facebook or Twitter page and expect a flood of friends and followers to descend on you. Reach out. Make comments on others' posts. Don't just expect them to come to you. Oh, and once they do come, don't forget to reciprocate. When someone posts on your wall, go and check it out there. You may not be able to do this every single time, but make it a practice and you will see your social media relationships blossom.

2. Don't dismiss someone's issue

Care about what they care about. If you are truly trying to connect on social media, you'll have things in common. If someone is talking about a problem they are having or something they really like, just as in a face-to-face relationship, don't dismiss it because you don't think it's important. It's important to THEM! I see so many people post a reply that belittles or makes light of a problem someone else is having. They wouldn't think to do this in person, so why do it on the Internet? People on the Internet are the same as they are in person. Their feelings and needs are not two dimensional just because they were read about online.

3. Don't trip over their conversation

This one's mostly for Facebook. If someone is making a point, don't nitpick them to death. Don't derail their conversation just as you wouldn't in real life. Unless something is really wrong, needs pointing out, or is just a request for opinions, don't hijack their conversation by talking about things that have very little to do with their point. If you feel strongly about that issue, post it on YOUR wall.

4. Don't make people look bad

If someone is trying to show how important something is, don't belittle it...or them. Don't post how silly it is. Look to see why they might be posting a note on that subject. I once saw someone post about how much they liked a particular product. One of their followers posted about how they didn't like it because it doesn't come in a particular color. In fact, they went so far as to post a link to one they liked better. Just out of curiosity, I looked at their bio and found that they sell them!

5. Don't rain on their parade

I don't know how many times I've seen someone post a funny Facebook note or quick Twitter quote about something and had someone take it too seriously. I've seen a rather curt response that implied that this person was making fun of something or someone. So many people these days are looking for something to be offended by so they can pick apart someone's light-hearted comment and their intent is fairly obvious. Pick your battles. I do think there are times when we should not sit idly by. However, even at those times, it is important that we address the issue with grace and respect.

6. Don't make fun of their serious issue

On the other side of the coin is the person who posts about a problem, and it won't win you any Facebook friends followers if you poke fun at their expense. I have seen where someone has posted about something of grave importance to them when someone posts a callous response. Mostly this is because they were not aware of the seriousness of the issue and have a humorous side to their personality. Its fine to joke, but you need to be able to discern when it will be taken well and when it won't. If you aren't sure, check their past posts, bio or links posted before and after this one. See if this doesn't give you a clue as to the nature of their issue. Be aware of any LOL's or D smiley faces in the post that suggest that this isn't really a dire issue.

7. Don't boldly go where some friend wouldn't go before!

If you know someone takes issue with a particular topic, don't invite them to that group, post that picture on their wall or make that comment. Know your audience. It's a communication term I use (and actually the title of a communication study I wrote for children) that helps to discern how to communicate effectively with different people. God didn t make cookie-cutter people so there is no one-size-fits-all way to communicate. I have had a few people post things on my wall, tag me in a note or reply to me on Twitter with links to things most people would know I wouldn't be interested in (if they had only looked at my bio or anything I post).

Contacting everyone (people who live all over the world) with an invitation to a party at your church is a bit silly and feels very impersonal to the recipient. Making reference to a woman's looks repeatedly when that woman is married will make her feel like you're a stalker! Be careful to tweet or post things that you would be comfortable saying to in person, face to face.

8. Don't ignore a friend

It isn't always possible to address each person individually. We're all busy and there may be just too many people replying to an issue to respond to each one. However, when someone makes a concerted effort to keep in touch by posting on your wall, replying to your posts, asking questions, etc., it's only polite to at least acknowledge them. Again, think of the same situation if it were taking place at a party at someone's house. You may be standing around in a crowd of 20 people all talking and laughing together. One man may make a comment or two that gets lost in the crowd, but if that same man asks a question of you at a moment when nobody happens to be talking, it's just rude not to answer him.

9. Don't take a friend for granted

Say thank you when someone goes out of their way to research something for you that you posted about. Reciprocate, especially when someone consistently takes the time to reply to you. Go looking for those who comment on your blog or always reply or come to your aide. Again, we have to think of our social media friends as we would our in-person friends. The same manners apply. Although I have seen where "real life" friends have been taken for granted after years of giving to a relationship; it is generally accepted that when someone does something nice for you, it's polite to acknowledge and thank them. However, online it can get lost and can feel so impersonal that sometimes people forget that this two-dimensional, black and white text post has behind it a real three-dimensional person with feelings. Don't forget your friends, especially the ones who go out of their way to reply, give you feedback, information and support.

10. Don't post insulting quizzes on their wall

You might think this is something most people wouldn't need to be told, but I have had so many people post one of those Facebook Friend Facts or Quiz things on my wall that ask things like, "Is JoJo a loose woman?", "Do you think JoJo is a drama queen?" and "Do you think JoJo lies?" Now if you are really good friends and you think this would be funny to them, you MIGHT post it. But do remember that even your good friends may have some Facebook friends reading along that don't know them. Would you say something like this at a party with folks around that you don't know very well?

The most important thing to remember about social media like Facebook and Twitter is that it is social. It's public and very much like a virtual party. Before you post anything, think who might see it, how it could be taken by those reading, especially since they do not have the benefit of your facial expressions, body language, tone of voice, eye contact and gestures. Remember, too, that they do not have the ability to converse with you in real time allowing them to ask questions for clarification.

SOCIAL MEDIA & INFLUENCER MARKETING

It seems unbelievable that over half of all small business owners did not make use of social media marketing in 2009. With Facebook reporting that they had 250 million people using their network (and Twitter not too far behind) in 2009, businesses should be stepping all over each other to get the best use of social media marketing.

The newsfeed on Facebook a user sees each time they refresh their home page plays a very influential role on the user's thoughts and activities. We see posts about the party that night, the great deal our friend got shopping, who's eating what and where, and which album is worth the money. It's undeniable that once we walk away from the computer, these thoughts are still floating around in our heads, waiting to be brought back up with another trigger.

Along the side of the newsfeed and every profile on Facebook, we see ads that have been tailored to us based on our likes and dislikes on Facebook. This has to be a business owner's dream come true. Not only do they have direct access to market their brand to us, but the technology behind Facebook will make your ad viewable by those who are most likely to buy from you.

So why didn't more businesses invest in social media marketing last year? The easy answer might be lack of technological knowledge. It might seem like a lot of work for business owners to set up profiles and run business from a computer screen. We are creatures of habit and the old way of TV and radio commercials seem safer because they have experience with it. But times are changing and every successful business owner knows that they must keep up.

That is why more businesses are planning to increase email marketing, use of social media marketing and decrease their use of TV and radio advertising. Out with the old in with the new for the New Year.

I can say, without a doubt that the businesses making this change will see substantial growth. I personally find myself leaning towards companies and brands I happen to see online. I also spend more time online than I do watching the TV or listening to the radio and I think that the greater population is with me. On a normal night, you can find me, a friend and my sister sitting in front of the television with our laptops on our laps. Our focus, during commercial breaks, is definitely on the Internet and not the TV.

A company that advertises online seems advanced and staying up with the times. We want to do business with smart, up-to-date people, not dinosaurs. To brand yourself, you have to get your company and its products online and viewable by as many people as possible. Facebook is a great starting place, as is Google and Twitter...and the list goes on.

As more and more companies get on the social media marketing bandwagon, we can expect more sites to emerge who will benefit from all the investments in online advertising. The Internet will be the primary place to influence consumer behavior. For businesses who want to stay at the forefront of influence marketing, now is the time to get on board with social media marketing.

5 Steps to Hack Your Facebook Influencer Marketing Campaign

Facebook is not only a platform to be used by the average Internet user anymore, but have also become a powerful tool for any type of business that wishes to be a success online. The platform features a variety of useful options and tools that businesses can now utilize to help them gain more recognition for their brands.

Facebook has more than two billion monthly active users. This is quite a significant number and it continues to grow by an average of around 17% year after year. Furthermore, approximately 1.15 billion Facebook account holders access the website from their mobile phone – as much as every single day.

It has been reported that as much as five new Facebook accounts are registered for every second of the day that passes. With so many users, it is obvious that here and there you will most definitely find a social media influencer in a variety of niches.

Now that we have looked at vital statistics about Facebook, let's switch our focus to how you can utilize influencer marketing on Facebook by considering a step-by-step process that will almost guarantee the success of such a campaign.

1. Focus on Improving Your Personal and Business Profiles

Even though you will be primarily directing traffic to your business profile on Facebook and also to your website, which is an external location, through the influencer marketing campaign, it does not mean people will not be able to see your personal profile as well. Thus it is important to spend time to clean up your personal profile and ensure it looks professional. Additionally, you need to make sure your business profile has been set up in an attractive way that represents your brand in a positive light.

2. Keep Posting on Your Facebook Business Page

One of the biggest mistakes you can make when it comes to Facebook influencer marketing is simply creating a new Facebook business page to represent your brand and immediately turning toward an influencer to gain more authority. Think about your reaction when you visit a Facebook page with no useful content – you immediately leave and search for another page that contains relevant information.

Thus, start out by creating some useful content and publishing the content on your Facebook business page. Once you have an adequate amount of posts to keep your visitors busy, you may think about moving on to influencers.

3. Always Plan Your Influencer Marketing Strategy

Planning for an influencer marketing strategy is very important. Improper planning may lead to excessive and unexpected costs, as well as the inability to truly utilize both the influencer and Facebook for the numerous benefits they feature when these two online marketing strategies are combined. While planning, define exactly what you expect from your influencer marketing strategy. Do you wish to reach more customers? Would you like to obtain more likes for your Business page or do you need to drive more traffic directly to your website?

You will need to establish the type of content you wish to promote; this could be text, images, videos or Facebook live, or a combination of them. This will be helpful in assisting you with finding the best influencer for your campaign. You should also note that defining your budget during this step can be very helpful.

4. Time to Find The Perfect Influencer

Once you have your planning in front of you, the next step is to find an influencer who you can use to fulfill your influencer marketing strategy. There are different ways to find potential influencers in your industry. Many Internet marketers, especially those on a smaller budget who cannot afford the expensive agency fees that hook a business owner up with an influencer, is by using the top search bar on Facebook to search for phrases related to their niche.

5. Now…Negotiate and Launch

The last step is to choose one of those influencers and then use them as part of your influencer marketing strategy. Make sure the influencer you choose falls within the criteria you have set previously and that you are able to afford them on the budget previously laid out. After negotiating with the influencer, you should send them the appropriate content to publish on their Facebook channel once again; the type of content will depend on your previous planning.

WAYS SOCIAL MEDIA INFLUENCERS CAN GROW YOUR BRAND

Are you considering introducing influencer marketing as part of your content strategy on Facebook, Instagram, or other social network? Brands have plenty to gain by engaging in influencer marketing. Working with the right influencers can have a multitude of positive effects on your brand's business. In this blog post, I'll share 8 reasons why influencer marketing can be a real asset. Let's go!

1. They Generate Sales

Of course, one of the main reasons brands seek out influencers is a means to generate sales. How you and an influencer decide to start edging people towards the sales funnel – and what part they might have in making sure customers' stay in it - will be between you and them. In a survey by Linqia of 170 marketers, 89 percent are happy with the authentic brand content created by social media influencers, 77 percent cite brand/product engagement as key benefits and 56 percent report traffic to websites and landing pages as a key payoff.

2. They're Inspirational Content Machines

There's good reason that influencers have large followings in the first place – they're passionate about their interests and have a proven track record at building and sharing content that resonates with their audience, expertise that you can tap into. By working with an influencer, you not only benefit from their reach but have the ability to share in their honed-in eye for successful social media posts, either on their profiles or your own. Even after a project is finished, you're sure to take away new ideas and strategies you can run with on your own.

3. They Build Brand Awareness

Generating sales might be the main goal of influencer marketing for many brands, but the brand awareness built within this process is unrivaled. After all, how can something like a static advert or a press release for a product or service compete with a real life person with a real enthusiasm talking about your brand to their audience? They're perfect as a middle man to communicate your brand's vision and message in a way that will encourage followers to engage and connect.

4. Their Voice is Trusted

As I mentioned in the introduction to this book, consumers are proven to trust the opinion of their peers and influencers more than a brand's message alone. According to a joint study by Twitter and analytics firm Annalect, 47 percent of respondents said they had purchased an item online after seeing it used by an influencer on Instagram, Twitter, Vine or YouTube.

5. They Can Offer Great ROI

When compared to traditional advertising and PR activity, collaborating with influencers still provides excellent value for money when your aim is to connect with a target market. In one study conducted by Tap influence, influencer marketing generated an unprecedented ROI. Working with White Wave Foods and Nielsen Catalina Solutions to track the in-store purchases exposed to influencer marketing, the results were staggering. They showed a total of $285 in incremental sales per 1000 impressions, some 11 times greater the expectations from a traditional digital advertising campaign. The study also revealed influencer marketing to be a surprisingly long tail, with new customers discovering the content months after the original post. Of course, this is likely to be the exception rather than the rule, but does show what can be achieved if you find the right influencer to showcase your brand in a way that resonates with your audience.

6. They Are Transparent and Reach Ad-Blind consumers

Assuming that you agree with influencers that your participation with them will be made clear within any sponsored content (and you should), transparent influencer marketing can provide a fresh way to reach a growing number of people who mistrust traditional digital advertising. Consumers are more likely to be receptive to a promotional message when it is made known that they are being targeted. In a study carried out by Harris Poll for Lithium Technologies in 2016 , 74% of Generation Z (16-19 year-olds) and millennials (20-39 year-olds) said they did not like being targeted by adverts via their social media feeds. However, while revealing that they are tired of being targeted and less receptive to adverts, 35% of 16-39 year olds also said that they trusted celebrity endorsements, and 50% trusted blogs.

7. They Become Brand Advocates

A one-and-done campaign with an influencer is perfectly all right, but if you develop a long-term relationship that goes beyond simple brand awareness and generating interest in your product, then the real value of having an influencer in your corner will show. The stronger your connection grows, the more your influencer will start to feel like a true brand ambassador, hopefully resulting in the kind of proud content that rubs off on your target audience.

8. They Can Grow Your Numbers

Beyond an over-arching goal like driving sales, influencers can also have the very welcome side effect of driving traffic to your website (by sharing your blog posts), increasing your social following (by tagging your brand in their posts), and improving your SEO – by back linking to your website on their blog, for example.

REASONS WHY INFLUENCER MARKETING IS GOOD FOR YOUR BUSINESS

Influencer marketing is a form of digital marketing that entirely focuses on building positive relationships and sentiments within your target audience through specific key individuals – the influencers. It's about attracting, building trust and generating engagement with the audience. Sounds like love relationship yeah? It is.

Your audience can enjoy and feel positive attributes for a brand and its product and as an end result, they build lasting and loyal relationships with the brands that serve them.

For many brands, though, connecting with a potential customer at this level is tough and time consuming. This is because consumers do not easily trust brands due to perceived bias. It can take a long time for brands to lead a consumer through the journey from the awareness stage to the final purchase.

Brands tend to need help with developing and organizing the sort of brand-customer relationship solely built on trust, and that's where influencer marketing takes center stage. Influencer marketing involves identifying the people who have the most influence on your target audience.

WHO IS AN INFLUENCER?

An Influencer is a third party who significantly shapes the customer's purchasing decisions and has a greater than average reach or impact in a relevant market place.

A highly-viewed youtuber or even a largely followed twitter user who has wowed their fans with appealing content is as much an influencer as a famous celebrity. You can read my story on how I became an Influencer. Hence, an influencer is defined based on the nature of the influencer marketing campaign, in order to reach the marketing goals. This may differ for each brand and campaign.

Influencers can encourage long-lasting customer loyalty by means of promoting engagement, appeal, and trus - the three attributes that result in long-term relationships and loyal customers. They use social media to achieve all these attributes. You can also read this article to learn more about how social media works and what you can do to grow.

WHY SHOULD YOUR BUSINESS CONSIDER INFLUENCER MARKETING?

BUILD AWARENESS AND ENGAGEMENT: Partnering with an influencer can help get your brand and products get in front of an engaged audience inquisitive about your product. An engaged target audience is an active target audience and influencers know how to get a response from their followers. In truth, within the past couple of years, influencers on Twitter and YouTube have been reaching a higher engagement rate than even famous celebrities.

GENERATE QUALITY LEADS: An influencer's actual testimony about your product can generate far more qualified leads than loads of ads, without all the additional marketing fees. The latest research indicates that influencer marketing has become the fastest developing customer acquisition channel, beating paid search, email marketing and organic search. Entrepreneurs were asked about the customers they generate through influencer marketing; 51 percent believed the leads generated are better than those attracted using other marketing strategies.

Working with influencers can also foster quality leads due to the fact that they exert their impact on specialized niches. Because of this specificity, the leads you generate from these influencers are more targeted and relevant. The result is a better number of leads who are already interested in what you sell.

BUILD TRUST AND BRAND AFFINITY: Trust is one of the most effective forces in the world of marketing. Trust between brands and customers can bring about a loyal relationship that outlasts the worst and most difficult of instances. Furthermore, an influencer who trusts your brand and your products might also become a brand ambassador. The influencers you partner with ought to clearly admire your products; and if so, this sentiment should be evident to their fans. When your influencers love and trust you, so will their followers.

Influencers are regular people with huge media reach - followers/fans, industry associations and community. Influencers may not necessarily be aware of your company, but they have influence over an audience segment that is important to your business.

Influencers are not just marketing tools, but social relationship assets. They could be responsible for affecting important contracts, product releases, market awareness and industry shifts before they happen.

THE BENEFITS OF SOCIAL INFLUENCER MARKETING

Word-of-mouth recommendations have long been recognized for their power and effectiveness and social influencer marketing takes this concept to the next level. The value it has for brands is supported by thenumbers. Ninety-two percent of people say they trust word-of-mouth recommendations over traditional advertising. That's an increase of nearly 20-percent from 2007 and is another reason why adept use of influencer marketing techniques provides a significant competitive advantage. Here is some important information on the value of social influencer marketing and how this strategy can pay dividends for your organization.

The Value of Social Influencers

Social influencers are people who possess the ability to modify the behavior and buying habits of others, either by shifting their opinions or providing them with new and actionable information.

Influencers are authorities in their communities — individuals who have the stature and gravitas necessary to put their weight and credibility behind something. They may be industry leaders, media members, scientists or bloggers. We frequently see high-profile celebrities, bloggers and influencers share their recommendations for products such as clothing, makeup, and travel on their social media profiles and blogs. An influencer's social media profile is prime real estate for brands to leverage a large, dedicated following to promote their products and services to an engaged audience.

Social influencers' biggest appeal to brands is their reach and loyal fan base. According to Adweek, food bloggers provide the highest ROI for brands, followed by fashion and travel. Influencers who possess sterling reputations and immense social reach wield enormous power. They are exceptionally valuable from a marketing perspective.

Penetrating Barriers

According to a survey, nearly half of all online consumers employ some kind of ad blocking software. But social influencer marketing deftly circumvents such barriers by providing the target audience with useful content from a respected authority. Ideally, consumers don't feel they are being sold anything, but instead are receiving well-thought out personal recommendations from a credible third party.

The Power of Your Audience

There are a few things to consider when using an influencer marketing campaign. First, you should assess the size of your influencer's audience versus the engagement of their posts. A larger network might not be as valuable as a smaller group that is passionately devoted. Keep in mind that influencers with more followers are typically much more expensive to work with compared to influencers with fewer followers due to the reach brands receive with a more prominent following.

It is also important to consider relevance. Influencers who are asked to market products outside their immediate community are not as effective. Finally, it is imperative to fully vet influencers you would like to work with since their followers need to align with your brand's target audience and core values. For instance, a brand wanting to push their newest protein bar might not want to partner with an influencer who frequently promotes trendy fast-food chains.

If you choose the right thought leaders, social influencer marketing can be a powerful tool to elevate your branding. You will increase your audience and potentially start a movement of loyal followers committed to your goals.

Over the last decade, social networks have brought remarkable transformations in our day-to-day lives. The rise of social media across the globe has revolutionized the way we communicate and share information. Not just personal lives, but social networking applications have made their way into the business world. Marketing through the social media channels is the new trend and every business organization is jumping onto this bandwagon. Influencer marketing revolves around the surging popularity of such social media channels. Before we delve into the details of this innovative marketing strategy, let's find out what an influencer is.

A person who is an industry expert and is respected for his opinion is known as an influencer. More than this, they are active online and have a number of followers. It can be a celebrity, journalist, bloggers oranalyst with in-depth expertise and credibility on a certain subject matter. When these respected individuals post anything about niche subject matters, it will be followed by a huge number of people. It can influence the purchase decisions of many customers. That is why business organizations need to incorporate influencer marketing techniques into their marketing mix. Platforms like Facebook, Twitter, Instagram and YouTube have led to the increasing popularity of a new generation influencers. A large number of people have amassed huge followers by uploading informative videos, online tutorials, easy hacks and more. When you hire the professional services of a reliable influencer marketing agency, they will help you connect with your targeted audience easily.

What are the major benefits of launching an influencer marketing campaign for your business? The primary advantage is its effectiveness.

Word of mouth recommendations are the best marketing tools for any business at any point of time. Influencer marketing is a type of digital word-of-mouth recommendation. It can have a great impact on the targeted audience. A blogger outreach tool and other techniques used by the influencers can grab the attention of your intended customer base easily.

An increase in search engine rankings is another important benefit. Building your brand through innovative brand management techniques and social media optimization strategies can increase the online visibility of your website. Last but not least, the influencer marketing method is trackable and targetable. Digital marketing techniques let you keep track of the activities and retrieve valuable insights about your advertising performance. These are only some of the major advantages of the influencer marketing method. So make it a point to find the right influencer in order to attain successful results.

THE IMPORTANCE OF SOCIAL MEDIA INFLUENCERS

These days, word-of-mouth and peer recommendations are more reliable to customers when it comes to brands. In simple words, if my friends trust or recommend a brand, then so will I. Mass advertisements are still paramount for their powerful reach, but they more often than not succeed in creating brand awareness alone. For customers to truly consider purchasing your products or services, personal approaches are necessary too. But it is obviously not possible for you to directly engage with innumerable potential customers. This is where social media influencers come in.

These "influencers" as they are called, are individuals who can sway the sentiments of their online audience in a particular direction regarding a brand, idea, business or person. And there just might be people out there who are already making or breaking the reputation of your brand and have the potential to help you increase your popularity. Let's take PepsiCo, the first brand to effectively use social media influencers, as an example. When the company decided to revamp its entire brand, it sent out cans bearing the new design to select bloggers, who then blogged about the changes resulting in brand awareness. But it didn't end there. These bloggers also influenced their audience to have a favorable attitude towards the change. So what made PepsiCo realize the importance of such influencers and why should you do the same?

1. Wide and Loyal Audience

Social media influencers generally have a large Twitter following, a long Facebook friends list or heavy blog traffic which means that through them you can reach a wide audience. If they mention your brand name, talk about it or retweet or share your posts, they are amplifying your brand communication.

2. Good Networks

Influencers build good networks. Their contacts engage in conversations or discussions on the various subjects the influencers post about, which can lead to more brand building. Not just that, they share or retweet these posts which means that your audience multiplies, increasing your visibility. Tugh them you can identify other influential people as well, who are a part of their audience. They can in turn influence their own audience's opinion of your brand. Influencers get the message across to the people in their network, who then send it to their own audience, resulting in a snowball effect thereby reaching out to a wider audience.

3. Content

In a survey conducted by Vocus and Brian Solis, 62% of the respondents said that they follow an influencer because of the content they create. Quality content is crucial to any marketing campaign. Influencers can create great content that would easily strike a chord with the audience, and reduce your work. They might even come up with creative ideas for content marketing that your brand did not think of. Some post reviews of your products and services, its features, quality etc., some write stories related to your brand, so on and so forth.

4. Credibility

Another important factor that contributes to their large following is credibility. In the same survey, 51% of the respondents said that they follow an influencer because they consider them as opinion leaders, and 40% follow them because of their relationship with the influencer.

The expertise these individuals hold in a particular field combined with the good relations they maintain with their audience makes them reliable. Their opinion of your brand will most likely become the general opinion of their audience. A word from an influencer can make or break your brand.

5. New Trends & Insights

Influencers are usually aware of the latest trends of the evolving social media platforms. They tend to be among the first to try these new trends, to discover new platforms to reach and engage with their audience. Through them, you too can get acquainted with such new ideas and employ them to interest prospective customers. Seeing as they are experts in the field, you could gain deeper insights about your industry from them.

More often than not, influencers fall under the category of lead users or early adopters. Marketers are heavily engaging social media influencers these days, and it is indeed important to identify them. Building good relationships with them will help strengthen their advocacy or convince them to become associated with your brand.

Identifying these influencers from the vast ocean of social media users is not an easy task. That's where social media listening comes in handy; tools such as Explic8 can help you identify your loyalists or even those who hate your brand. You can not only identify the top authors in terms of numbers but also measure their influence and categorize them as your promoters or detractors, and engage with them in real time.

STEPS TO EFFECTIVE INFLUENCER MARKETING

People trust recommendations from third-party sources even more than the brand itself. This is, in essence, why influencer marketing exists. Influencer marketing is, in a nutshell, when marketers look for, identify, and engage with influencers. There's an increasing trend of brands making use of influencer marketing, and understandably so: when you engage with influencers, not only do they raise awareness, but they also encourage and raise action among their audience and their network. They can increase your online exposure, and in some cases you may find that they can sell your products even better than you do.

While more brands are adopting this type of marketing, don't do it just because others are doing it, but only in support of a business objective. This will give you a direction and an indication of which influencer(s) to target. Influencer marketing consists of 3 main steps:

- Identifying influencers

- Target said influencers

- Market to, with, and through those influencers

Before we move into each point, we need to clarify a few things about influencers:

In-depth: What is an influencer and what does he/she do?

Simply put: An influencer is anyone who has the power to affect something or someone. In reality, we all have some influence. Every day we exercise our influence, sometimes unknowingly – whether it's at work, home, in our personal lives, or online. However, while we may all be influential, we're not all influential in the same topic or area. For instance, while I may have some influence in digital marketing, I'm not influential to a fashion company looking for a fashion blogger for London Fashion Week. This is when relevancy comes into place – because of relevancy, not every influencer is your influencer.

Even within your own target market, there are many types of influencers:

- opinion leaders

- analysts

- experts

- predictors

- critics

- trendsetters

- creators/starters

- decision makers

- celebrities

- and many, many more

Ultimately, in terms of marketing, you have 5 main types of influencers, which I illustrated in the diagram below:

Sector Influencers

These are influencers within your sector. They usually have a large following and are looked up to as experts in your target market.

Aim: these influencers may or may not be aware of your brand (especially if you're up and coming or you lack exposure), so it's your job to market to them.

Brand influencers: these are people who have an influence around your brand on other people or on the brand itself.

Aim: these influencers have the power to attract people to your brand or detract people from it.

Not all influencers work in your favor. Some have a positive influence on your brand (positive influencers), while others have the power to take people away from your network (negative influencers). The latter are commonly known as "brand detractors".

Within positive brand influencers, you have a group of influencers called "brand advocates": these works as an "unofficial extension" of your brand, as they work in your favor without being on your payroll.

The next level up (and possibly the ultimate level of advocacy) from a brand influencer is "brand ambassador". Brand ambassadors represent your brand, whether they work for it or not.

To get started, we need to identify influencers:

Who are your influencers? These are not only people who talk about you online, but people who influence other people by what they say and what they share about you.

Depending on your sector and your brand, you might have hundreds or maybe thousands of influencers online. So, how do you find them?

The first step is social listening. Use queries to find who's talking about you. Your queries will depend on who you're looking for and what type of influencer you're looking for – a sector influencer, or a brand influencer.

If you're looking for a sector influencer, look for:

- people talking about your target market

- people talking about your competitors

- people talking (in general) about products and services you offer

If you're looking for a brand influencer, look for:

- people talking about your brand
- people talking about your products
- people sharing your content

When building your queries, think about the topics your influencers would write about, the type of content they would read and share, what keywords and hashtags they would use when talking about your subject area. For example, if they're into social media marketing, they're likely to use hashtags like #smm or #social, and you may often find them active in various Twitter chats or Google Hangouts. Before you can work with an influencer, you need to think like one.

You can find both free and paid tools to search for people talking about you, but bear in mind that the quality of the tool you use has an impact on the quality of results you get. A few great tools I definitely recommend are Brandwatch (paid), Crimson Hexagon (paid), Synthesio (paid), and Hootsuite (free and paid). The choice is ultimately yours. Now, while I'm not going to get into the nitty-gritty details of social listening tools and their requirements, here are some of the main features to look for in a social listening tool for influencer marketing:

Sources: make sure your social listening tool can search in the sources you need. The main ones you'll need are social networks (not only the usual suspects, e.g. Twitter, Facebook, Reddit, but also other networks you wouldn't normally think of like Flickr,

Instagram, Pinterest, LinkedIn, Tumblr etc.), blogs, forums and discussion boards. It's useful to have a tool that can look into "mainstream sources", such as online newspapers, company sites, and online zines.

URL search: your tool needs to be able to look for various links and domains. For instance, you may want to find people sharing your most recent blog post or a specific page from your website (URL search), but you need to be aware of people sharing any link from your website.

Most people use a URL shortener that will shorten your links for them (e.g. bit.ly, po.st); others use apps to do it for them (e.g. Hootsuite, Buffer). Either way, a number of social listening tools don't support searches for shortened links. If this is a deal-breaker for you, make sure you ask your account manager before you acquire a social listening tool.

Ranking: most tools offer some sort of influence ranking for every piece of content they find for you. Some tools integrate with other influence ranking platforms (e.g. Brandwatch with Kred), while others have their own in-house ranking algorithm (e.g. Synthesio with SynthesioRank).

Sentiment: while you want to find influencers, you need to segment the chatter around your brand (or your target market) by sentiment. Not all chatter is good, but even negative mentions of your brand can be helpful, as you can often turn the situation around in your favor. Social sentiment is a touchy subject for everyone in digital marketing, and I've already discussed why that is such an intricate subject.

Ranking influencers

Now that you've gotten your search results, you have two groups to look at: content from people talking about you, and content from influencers. While you should target both groups in your marketing strategy, you shouldn't do it in the same manner. So how do you spot a brand influencer? Look out for these three main points:

Relevancy: is this person relevant to your brand? If they were to tweet about your brand, would their network find it believable, or would it be out of context?

Reach: how big is this person's audience? Influencers often have large social audiences and are part of social communities, whether they're an influential voice within the community or at the forefront. On the other hand, you also have "micro-influencers", people who may not have a large audience but they're people to whom your audience goes when making decisions about your brand (whether to buy your products, etc.).

Impact: how is this person perceived? Is (s)he perceived as an authoritative and/or knowledgeable person? How persuasive is he in his network? Now that you've filtered your influencers, you need to sort them by your own influence ranking. This may differ from brand to brand. Ultimately, make sure you're looking at the following qualities:

Sentiment: what is this person's sentiment towards your brand or your target market?

Reach: how big is their audience? How far does their influence go?

Affiliation: are they affiliated with some other company (e.g. your competitor), or are they creating content independently?

Impact: how persuasive and influential are they in their network? How often is their content shared, and what is people's perception of it?

Experience: how experienced are they in your target market or brand?

Remember, not all influencers are the same. While the common perception of an online influencer is that they're chatty and they constantly talk about their expertise, this is not always the case. You'll often find people who are an expert in a subject area but they remain silent about it until asked by people who view them as a great resource of information.

Working with influencers:

You've found the real influencers now what?

The first step is thank them. This is the starting point in a potential relationship between you and them, and it shows them that you acknowledge their contribution, as well as their passion, expertise, and the time they've spent talking about your or sharing your content to their network. Treat them as your partners.

Now, while you can't force your influencers to talk about you, you can always encourage the idea. Don't be pushy, as it's quite easy to turn a brand advocate into a detractor. You can do so in many ways. Engage them and ask their opinion on a new feature, service or product you're launching, or an existing one. Give them an incentive for producing content, whether it's a gift, a giveaway, a discount, or some sort of "loyal member" status that they can wear proudly. Encourage any type of content creation it doesn't necessarily have to be a blog post. Anything from an Instagram photo to a YouTube video and a Vine can help.

See where they're engaged and, if you see fit, engage there too perhaps they have regular Twitter chats they attend, or Google Hangouts they follow be present. Take it offline have conversations with these influencers by email, but go one step further – meet them offline if possible, or arrange for that to be possible.

Be their partner make them feel special, and dare I say give them a special treatment, because brand advocates are those who will talk about your brand when unsolicited. I've been given trials before without any sort of financial or contractual commitment, and in return I've written reviews about the products out of my own will only because these brands see me as influential in their subject area and as a strong advocate for their brand.

How to repay influencers:

Unless this brand advocate is being paid to share your content, they're not doing what they do to help you as a brand, but to help their network. Influencers thrive in helping their large pool of connections with genuine content and helpful information. What you offer them depends largely on the task and on how they work – accepting or rejecting your offer is entirely their prerogative.

There are ultimately three ways you could compensate your influencers:

Financially: this will be at your and the influencer's discretion, and it's often the case for freelancers.

Discount/Giveaway: as a substitute for money, you could always give away something from your brand to your influencer. A brand advocate will appreciate this and it may keep them talking about you during (and often after) the lifetime of what you're giving away.

Moral Incentive: this could be a promise of sharing their content to your network (especially if you have a very large following).

Speaking of moral incentive: increasing your influencer's exposure is not always a valid form of payment, and some people may find it offensive (especially if they see that you do have enough money and are choosing not to pay them). There are plenty of stories online of great freelancers who have gone through this. As your brand influencer is working for you as an unofficial extension of your brand, it is only fair that you keep their best interests in mind before your own profit.

Build influencers:

Influencer marketing is a work in progress. There will always be new people talking about you, whether positively or negatively. If you start with this exercise, make it a continuous one. You can easily do this with the help of Hootsuite or Tweet deck, so you can see what people are saying about you in real time.

Make sure that finding influencers isn't just for an internal report but it's to reach out, acknowledge and engage with them. You too can contribute to this whenever you create genuine moments; they can trigger brand advocacy, sometimes when you least expect it.

THE ESSENCE OF INFLUENCER FOR BUSINESS GROWTH

Think about the last new product you tried and how you found out about it. Did someone tell you about it? Did you google it or go to its website to see what people had to say? Ask a friend about it?

My guess is that at some point before you purchased it, someone recommended it to you. That someone could have been your friend or family member, your favorite social media influencer, a trusted expert, a credible media outlet or even another brand or organization you trust.

Every other year, Nielsen comes out with its Trust in Advertising report, and "recommendations from friends or family" is always the number one trusted source of information, closely followed by company websites, consumer reviews and editorial articles.

Whenever we make a decision to spend your money on something unproven, we seek some kind of proof or assurance that it will be a quality and good experience, which is why we rely on what other people say about it.

It used to be that media outlets and review sites were the only places to find recommendations, but now anyone can become a social media influencer and a megaphone for your brand.

Influencer marketing has been on the rise. In the last two years, "influencer marketing" as a search term on Google Trends has risen by 400%. Companies both big and small are realizing the power of building relationships with influencers.

Especially for startups and new businesses looking to build their brand credibility, it is important to find people and organizations with whom you can align. The great thing about influencer marketing is that you can kill three birds with one stone:

1. Create great content

2. Earn credibility

3. Gain exposure through their network

So how do you actually get influential people to talk about your business? Many people think you can just ask someone to talk about your product and they'll do it, but it doesn't work like that. You either need to compensate them for their time, spend months building a relationship, or provide something of value. Here are five ways you can start engaging influencers today:

Create a Valuable Experience

Influencers have built their reputation by meeting other people of influence. If you create an experience that allows influencers to network with other influencers, you will have the opportunity to build a personal relationship with them and share information about your product, and maybe they will talk about it on social media. However, this shouldn't be the goal. The goal should be to raise awareness for what you do and start to build a relationship with them that might net something in the future.

Offer Exposure

Influencers have built their following by getting exposure talking about what they love. Ask them if they would be willing to do a 30-minute interview for a blog post or to come to your office for a Facebook Live Chat. This approach works best when you have already built up a following on your own social channels to make sure it is worth their time. In an ideal world, they will share the blog post or promote the Facebook Live on their channels and help attract new potential customers for you.

Ask For Advice

Influencers like sharing their thoughts on books, blogs, events, etc. Ask them if they would be willing to serve as an advisor to your business with other like-minded influencers. You can host virtual or in-person quarterly meetings to get their perspective on relevant trends in the marketplace and customer needs while getting feedback on the direction your business is headed.

Hire As A Spokesperson or Speaker

Hire a high-profile influencer to serve as a media spokesperson or a speaker at a customer event. This approach allows you to borrow equity from an established expert in the space who isn't motivated to sell, so it creates a more valuable experience for the audience. When hiring a spokesperson or speaker, it's best that you identify someone who authentically supports what you do and build a relationship before any speaking engagements. You'll want to share messages about your business with them in advance, but let them put the messages into their own words so they can authentically share their opinion.

Pay For A Product Review

The fastest and most straight-forward way to engage an influencer is to pay them to create content. This works best for consumer products looking to work with bloggers, Instagrammers, etc. While you may be compensating them to create content, it is important to give them editorial freedom to ensure that the post they create feels authentic to their audience. This is a great example of a sponsored post done well by Mommy Shorts. While the post is sponsored by Land of Nod, it is her personal description of the entire experience that makes it attention-grabbing, trustworthy and helps position Land of Nod as a company to buy from.

CONCLUSION

Facebook is the world's largest social media network, boasting over two billion monthly active users. The network allows for the sharing of virtually any content type, including text, image, and video, and features a variety of offerings that businesses can take advantage of to help them gain a competitive advantage in their industries. When utilizing an influencer in your industry on Facebook, you are instantly gaining access to a new target audience, garnering more trust for your brand and driving more potential customers to your website.

Connecting with influencers takes time. Don't expect a relationship to come from nothing, and don't give up too easily. One key element of Influence Marketing is earning the attention and respect of influencers, and that takes work.

Now you just have to start drawing up a plan for launching a successful Facebook influence campaign.

www.ingramcontent.com/pod-product-compliance
Lightning Source LLC
Chambersburg PA
CBHW070215230526
45471CB00002B/951